God's Good Gifts

A Scrapbooking Bible Study
for Women's Groups

Group's Scripture Scrapbooks™

Group
Loveland, Colorado

Group resources actually work!

This Group resource helps you focus on **"The 1 Thing™"**—a life-changing relationship with Jesus Christ. "The 1 Thing" incorporates our **R.E.A.L.** approach to ministry. It reinforces a growing friendship with Jesus, encourages long-term learning, and results in life transformation, because it's:

Relational
Learner-to-learner interaction enhances learning and builds Christian friendships.

Experiential
What learners experience through discussion and action sticks with them up to 9 times longer than what they simply hear or read.

Applicable
The aim of Christian education is to equip learners to be both hearers and doers of God's Word.

Learner-based
Learners understand and retain more when the learning process takes into consideration how they learn best.

God's Good Gifts
A Scrapbooking Bible Study for Women's Groups

Visit our Web site: **www.group.com**

Credits
Creative Development Editor: Matt Lockhart
Chief Creative Officer: Joani Schultz
Editor: Beth Robinson
Copy Editor: Alison Imbriaco
Art Director: Kari K. Monson
Cover Art Director: Jeff A. Storm
Cover Designer: Jane Parenteau
Photographer: Rodney Stewart
Scrapbook Samples: Cris Alsum and Kari K. Monson
Production Manager: Peggy Naylor

ISBN 0-7644-2646-X

10 9 8 7 6 5 4 3 2   13 12 11 10 09 08 07

Printed in Malaysia.

We are deeply grateful to the following women whose devotions add so much to this book.

Kay Arthur

Emilie Barnes

Jill Briscoe

Jody Brolsma

Sherri Harris

Amy Nappa

$\mathcal{W}$elcome to *God's Good Gifts*—the third book in Group's Scripture Scrapbooks™ series. This book will provide another opportunity for you and a small group of women to bring your memories together with God's Word for a time of fellowship, study, introspection, and meditation.

The more we grow in our relationships with God, the more we realize how good God has been to us. God gives us so many good gifts every day. You'll spend the next twelve weeks celebrating God's gracious and generous nature. You'll discover just how much God loves you as you think about how he's blessed your life through your family, your friends, and your church and by the way he's specially created you to be a unique and wonderful woman. In this book, you'll explore these gifts from God:

- Myself
- Church
- Home
- Rest
- Fun
- Freedom in Christ
- God's World
- My Purpose
- Children
- Sisterhood
- Family
- My Relationship With God

It is our hope that you'll have both a greater appreciation for yourself and a greater appreciation for your Lord and Creator at the end of this time together. Enjoy building friendships with other women, and don't be afraid to fully enjoy discovering who you are and who you can be through the Holy Spirit.

This book includes devotions, Scriptures, and prayers to help you discover all you can about God's good gifts to you. It also includes memory-making activities to do with your family and friends, activities to help you make memories with God, and scrapbooking tips and ideas. The book suggests a Scripture reading for each day of the week leading up to your group meeting. These Scriptures will deepen your understanding of the topic and help you get the most from your discussions with your friends.

Have fun with this book, and may it help you better love yourself, others, and the God who made you!

How Scripture Scrapbooking Works

As part of a Group's Scripture Scrapbooks™ group, you'll meet with other women every week for a time of Bible study and scrapbooking.

First you'll read the week's devotion and Scriptures together and then discuss the questions. Next you'll use the devotion pages from this book as the beginning of the two scrapbook pages you'll design and create each week. The devotions are designed to be torn out and placed in your scrapbook.

Each session you'll bring photos that relate to the week's topic. You can look ahead each week to know what pictures to bring the following week. This will give you time to make copies or to enlarge or reduce your photos to fit on your pages.

The templates from this book will help you create the second of the two pages you'll make each week. The templates are designed to lie on top of your photos so that you can see what you will be cutting out. To trace the photos, use a wax pencil designed for drawing on photos. Then the excess can be wiped off with a tissue after cutting. Make sure you have all the pictures laid out so you can see how the page will look before you actually cut any of the pictures.

There are many choices that can be made here; simple is just as acceptable as ornate. You'll find that sometimes the pages you create are fun and frivolous; other times they are deeply rooted with meaning.

There are many ways that the templates can be used. These are just a few ideas.

Supply List

Here are the supplies you'll need:

❏ *God's Good Gifts* participant book

❏ 8½x11 or 12x12 scrapbook

❏ scissors

❏ tape runner or acid-free adhesive of some kind

❏ wax pencil (to draw on photos)

Other supplies can include:

❏ a straightedge paper cutter (for greater precision on photos)

❏ decorative paper or card stock

❏ decorative scissors

❏ decorative pens

❏ stickers

❏ die cuts

❏ rubber stamps and stamp pads

❏ whatever else you want to make your scrapbook exclusively yours!

Remember, these scrapbooks are keepsakes for you to cherish and hold dear. Your scrapbook doesn't need to be a replica of someone else's, unless that is what you choose. It can be decorated without a lot of expense, and you can go back and add extras later.

Here are some ideas to get you started.

Myself
8½x11 sample

Home
12x12 sample

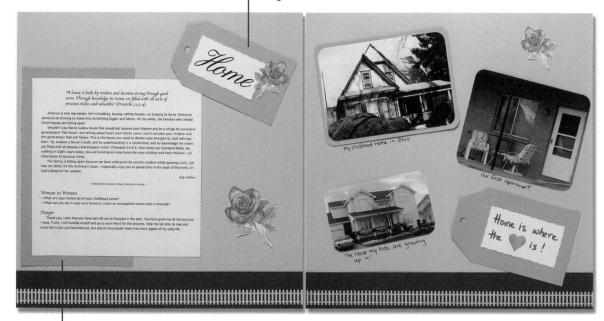

• Use the template shapes as journaling space.

• The gift tag template can remind us that everything is a gift from God.

• Photocopy devotion onto vellum so design shows through.

• Use light colored gel pens to write on dark background paper.

• Accent the devotion with an offset, solid color to make it stand out.

Idea Pages

Rest *8½x11 sample*

My Purpose *12x12 sample*

- Use printed background paper to accentuate the theme of the devotion.

- Colorful die cuts can pick up colors from your photos.

- Mulberry paper color can reflect a prominent color in your photos.

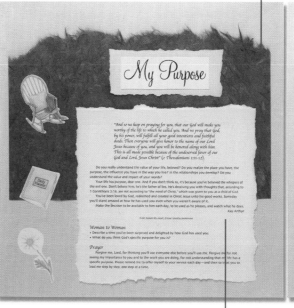

- Photocopy devotion and title onto vellum so design shows through.

- Different shapes of photographs add interest.

- Torn edges on the devotion accent the mulberry paper treatment.

Children
12x12 sample

Sisterhood
8½x11 sample

• Photos grouped very closely help reflect the high activity level of the day.

• Odd numbers of photos can be more interesting then even numbers.

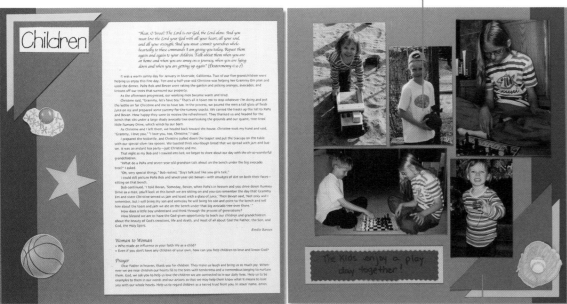

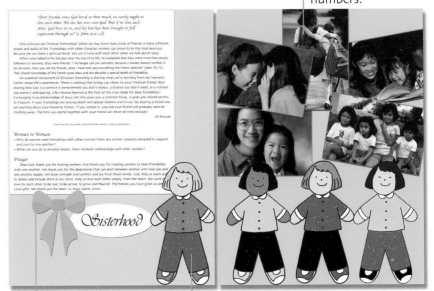

• Layered corner treatments add depth.

• Using different shades of paper adds dimension.

• Decorate to remind you of women who mean a lot to you.

Week 1: *Myself*

Use these activities throughout the week *before* your group meets to discuss this topic and scrapbook together. You'll find that meditating and praying on these topics each day of the week will draw you closer to God and increase your appreciation for his gifts.

Daily Bible Readings
Day 1: Read Psalm 139:1-4. How do you feel about God knowing everything about you?

Day 2: Read Psalm 139:13-16. What specifically is wonderful about you?

Day 3: Read James 2:8. What assumption does this verse make? In what ways is it appropriate to love yourself?

Day 4: Read Ephesians 4:22-24. What appropriate limits are there to loving yourself?

Day 5: Read 1 Corinthians 6:20. What does this verse say about your worth to God? How does that affect the way you see yourself?

Day 6: Read Psalm 8. How does the way God values people affect how you feel about yourself?

Family Memory Maker
Play a game with your family. Sit in a circle on the floor, and take turns spinning a bottle. Whoever the bottle is pointing to when it stops spinning must say something he or she likes about him- or herself. Keep playing until all family members have had a turn to spin and a turn to say something about themselves.

Personal Memory Maker
Spend some time thinking about the different stages of your life and the experiences that you have had, both good and bad. What are the stories of your life? What events have shaped you into the person you are today? Identify four or five events that have had a profound effect on you. Consider writing these experiences in story form. You may want to include these stories in your scrapbook.

Scrapbooking Tip
Make this week's scrapbook pages a celebration of you. Gather your favorite pictures of yourself to put in your scrapbook. Also gather small items that reflect your personality and your interests and hobbies. Use background papers in your favorite colors. Write a letter to God to thank him for creating you just as you are, and mount the letter in your scrapbook.

"When I look at the night sky and see the work of your fingers—
the moon and the stars you have set in place—
what are mortals that you should think of us,
mere humans that you should care for us?
For you made us only a little lower than God,
and you crowned us with glory and honor" (Psalm 8:3-5).

One evening our seven-year-old grandson, Chad, was helping me set the dinner table. Whenever the grandchildren come over, we have a tradition of honoring someone at the table with our red plate that says, "You Are Special Today"...It was natural for me to ask Chad, "Who should we honor today with our special plate?" Chad said, "How about *me*?" "Yes, Chad, you are special," I replied, "It's your day."

He was so proud as we all sat around the table and said our blessing. Then Chad said, "I think it would be very nice if everyone around the table would tell me why they think I'm special." Bob and I got a chuckle out of that, but we thought it might be a good idea, so we did it. After we were all through, Chad said, "Now I want to tell you why I think I'm special. I'm special because I'm a child of God." Chad was so right on. Psalm 139:13-14 tells us that God knew us before we were born. He knit us together in our mother's womb and we are wonderfully made.

When I was seven, ten, or even twenty-two, I could not have told anyone why I was special. I didn't even talk, I was so shy. My alcoholic father would go into a rage, swearing and throwing things. I was afraid I'd say the wrong thing, so I didn't talk. My self-image wasn't too good. But the day came when I read Psalm 139, and my heart came alive with the realization that I, too, am special because I am a child of God. And so are you. We were uniquely made as he knit us together in our mother's womb.

Verse 16 says [that] all the days are "ordained for me" (New International Version). It's not by accident you are reading this devotion today. Perhaps you, too, need to know how very special you are. We have all been given unique qualities, talents, and gifts. And you, my dear one, have been made by God. You are his child. He loves you more than any earthly father could possibly love you. Because he is your heavenly father, almighty God, he cares for you even when you don't care for yourself. You are his child even when you feel far from him. It's never your heavenly father who moves away from you. It's you who moves away from him.

Today is ordained by God for you to draw near to him and allow him to be near to you. Because today is your day, my friend, "You Are Special Today." A child of God, as Chad said.

Emilie Barnes

From *15 Minutes Alone With God*. Used by permission.

Woman to Woman
- What do you especially like about yourself?
- Why do you think God made you the way you are?

Prayer
Dear God, thank you for the gift of self. You have created each of us to be unique. We look different from each other. What we think is different from what others think. We all have individual dreams and passions, hurts and sorrows. We lead such different lives. Thank you, God, for the opportunity to live a life unlike anyone else's existence. Thank you for the chance to serve you in our own special ways. Help us not to take our individuality for granted, but rather let us celebrate our unique qualities as we each strive to serve you with wholehearted devotion. In Jesus' name, amen.

Week 2: *Church*

Use these activities throughout the week *before* your group meets to discuss this topic and scrapbook together. You'll find that meditating and praying on these topics each day of the week will draw you closer to God and increase your appreciation for his gifts.

Daily Bible Readings

Day 1: Read Romans 12:4-5. What is your function in the body of Christ? Are you fulfilling your role?

Day 2: Read Ephesians 4:11-16. Why is it so striking that the goal for the church is to grow and build itself up in love? Is your church growing toward this goal?

Day 3: Read 1 Peter 2:4-5, 9-10. In what ways do these verses inspire you? How do they affect your perspective on the church?

Day 4: Read 1 Corinthians 1:10. Is your church perfectly united in mind and thought? What can you do to promote unity in your church body?

Day 5: Read Colossians 1:15-18. What does it mean to say that Christ is the head of the church? How does that affect how we "do" church?

Day 6: Read Ephesians 5:22-27. How does this imagery affect how we understand the church?

Family Memory Maker

If your church has a directory, look through the directory together and identify the people you know. Identify how the people you know reflect Christ in their lives. Also notice people you don't know. Pick someone you don't know but would like to know. Have your family watch for that person the next time you're at church. Invite him or her out for lunch with your family, and spend some time making a new friend. Pray with your family to thank God for your church.

Personal Memory Maker

Take a drive, and look at the church buildings in your town or region. What can you surmise about each congregation from its building, grounds, and location? Consider how the various churches in your community represent God. How is God's church active and thriving? Where is it struggling? Thank God for the churches in your area. Pray for each congregation as you drive by its building, and ask God to strengthen his church.

Scrapbooking Tip

Use colored vellum to create "stained-glass" windows for this page. Cut window shapes out of sturdy paper, and cut openings in each of the windows. Cut colored vellum a quarter of an inch larger than the window opening, and use adhesive to attach the vellum to the inside of the opening. Attach pictures of people from your church to your page. Use adhesive along the left edge of the windows to attach them to the page so that the windows cover the people pictures. Leave the right side unattached so you can "open" the window and see the people inside. You may want to add a score line along the left edge of the windows to make it easier to open them.

Church

*"Without wavering, let us hold tightly to the hope we say we
have, for God can be trusted to keep his promise. Think of ways
to encourage one another to outbursts of love and good deeds.
And let us not neglect our meeting together, as some people do,
but encourage and warn each other, especially now that the day
of his coming back again is drawing near"* (Hebrews 10:23-25).

As a boy of twelve, Jesus had said to his parents, who had been looking for him, "You should have known that I would be in my Father's house" (Luke 2:49). Jesus' focus in life—even as a young man—was his Father's business. This is what he was about.

What are we about—our things or his things? Jesus' "things" included being in the temple listening and asking questions (Luke 2:46). Years later he taught in the synagogues (Luke 4:14-15). When he went to his hometown, Nazareth, "He went as usual to the synagogue on the Sabbath" (Luke 4:16).

If we, like our Lord and the apostle Paul, want to be doing God's business, we, too, must meet with a body of believers. We will never find a perfect church, and if we do, we should be careful not to join it, lest we spoil it! We should make our presence felt in our church! If the church is a group of God's people, God promises that he will be there. He said, "For where two or three gather together because they are mine, I am there among them" (Matthew 18:20).

Fellowship is a very important part of our spiritual life, for it keeps our faith burning. If a coal falls out of a fire, it will soon go out. Believers need to be an active part of a local church. As we focus individually and collectively on God's things, God is pleased.

Jill Briscoe

From *The One Year Book of Devotions for Women*. Used by permission.

Woman to Woman
• What do you have to gain from being a part of a church?
• What does the church have to gain from your participation?

Prayer
Father God, we thank you for the church. We thank you because we have a place to go and celebrate you. We thank you for the church body—the group of Christians who seek to serve you and love you. Our churches aren't perfect; it's easy to find things to complain about. But there's also so much to be thankful for. Thank you for the joy of singing together with others who love you. Thank you for the comfort of praying for one another and having others pray for us. Thank you for dear Christian people who teach us by their example and their words. Thank you for the opportunity to open your Word and study with others. We aren't alone. We have friends. We have the church. In Jesus' name, amen.

Week 3: *Home*

Use these activities throughout the week *before* your group meets to discuss this topic and scrapbook together. You'll find that meditating and praying on these topics each day of the week will draw you closer to God and increase your appreciation for his gifts.

Daily Bible Readings

Day 1: Read Matthew 7:24-27. What have you done to build your home on the rock?

Day 2: Read Proverbs 31:10-31. What lessons about home can you glean from these verses?

Day 3: Read Acts 16:13-15. How can you use your home to serve God?

Day 4: Read Proverbs 14:26. Is this true of your home? What can you do to make your home a secure fortress and a refuge for those who live there?

Day 5: Read Acts 2:46. How can our homes help us develop fellowship with one another?

Day 6: Read Isaiah 32:18. Why is this promise from God so pleasant and beautiful?

Family Memory Maker

Gather with your family, and talk about what you love about your home. Perhaps someone in your family loves the way you all cuddle under quilts to watch movies, or perhaps someone enjoys a holiday meal that you serve every year. Talk about God's wonderful gift of home. Make it a point this week to do some of the things your family enjoys.

Personal Memory Maker

One day this week, take a walk through your home. Remember the day you moved in and what your life was like then. As you enter each room, think about what happens in that room and the people who gather there. Pray in every room of your house, and ask God to bless and protect your family and all that happens in your home.

Scrapbooking Tip

This is a great time to use pictures of houses that you've lived in through the years. Consider handlettering this verse on your page: "As for me and my house, we will serve the Lord" (Joshua 24:15, King James Version).

Home

"A house is built by wisdom and becomes strong through good sense. Through knowledge its rooms are filled with all sorts of precious riches and valuables" (Proverbs 24:3-4).

America is into real estate. We're building, buying, selling houses—or longing to do so. Everyone seems to be striving to move into something bigger and better. All the while, the families who inhabit these houses are falling apart.

Wouldn't you like to build a house that would last beyond your lifetime and be a refuge for successive generations? The house I am talking about bears your family name, and it includes your children and the generations that will follow. This is the house you need to devote your energies to. God tells you how: "By wisdom a house is built, and by understanding it is established; and by knowledge the rooms are filled with all precious and pleasant riches" (Proverbs 24:3-4, New American Standard Bible). By walking in God's ways today, you are building an inheritance for your children and their children—an inheritance of spiritual riches.

The family is falling apart because we have embraced the world's wisdom while ignoring God's. Get into the Bible; it's the Architect's plans. I especially urge you to spend time in the book of Proverbs; it's God's blueprint for wisdom.

Kay Arthur

Woman to Woman
- What are your memories of your childhood home?
- What can you do in your own home to create an atmosphere where God is honored?

Prayer
Thank you, Lord, that you have not left me to flounder in the dark. You have given me all the direction I need, if only I will humble myself and go to your Word for the answers. Help me not only to read and study the truths you have laid out, but also to incorporate them into every aspect of my daily life. Amen.

Devotion and prayer from *Search My Heart, O God*. Used by permission.

Week 4: *Rest*

Use these activities throughout the week *before* your group meets to discuss this topic and scrapbook together. You'll find that meditating and praying on these topics each day of the week will draw you closer to God and increase your appreciation for his gifts.

Daily Bible Readings

Day 1: Read Matthew 11:28-30. What kind of rest does Christ offer?

Day 2: Read Psalm 55:4-8. When have you felt like this? What do you do when you feel this desperate?

Day 3: Read Genesis 2:1-3 and Exodus 34:21. Why do you think God took a day to rest? Why does God tell us to rest on the seventh day?

Day 4: Read Isaiah 26:3. What's the connection between trust and peace?

Day 5: Read Psalm 3:5 and 4:8. Is your sleep restful and peaceful? Why can those who follow God sleep in peace?

Day 6: Read Psalm 127:2. What does this verse say about rest?

Family Memory Maker

Observe a Sabbath rest with your family. For one day this week, simply rest. Don't run errands; don't do chores; don't even cook meals. Instead, spend time with your family or with friends. Go for a walk, enjoy a park together, visit a museum, go to a sporting event, or read books. For meals, consider eating sandwiches, or prepare a meal the day before so that you can simply reheat it. If you can't manage a full day of rest, at least do an afternoon or an evening.

Personal Memory Maker

Take a short personal retreat one evening this week. Take a hot bath. Add Epsom salts* to relax your muscles and an essential oil that you enjoy. Play relaxing music. Turn out the lights, and light several candles. While you soak, enjoy a talk with God. Don't feel the need to pray intensely, just enjoy a chat with him. Be sure to thank God for giving you rest.

Don't use Epsom salts if you have high blood pressure. Use bubble bath instead.

Scrapbooking Tip

What says rest to you? A nap in a big featherbed? A steaming mug of cocoa and a mystery novel? A long walk along a country lane? Find items that remind you of rest, such as a square of flannel from your favorite old nightgown, a picture of your favorite novel, or leaves from a tree by your favorite place to walk. Seal each item in a small archive-safe plastic bag, and attach the bags to your pages.

Rest

> *"Have you never heard or understood? Don't you know that the Lord is the everlasting God, the Creator of all the earth? He never grows faint or weary. No one can measure the depths of his understanding. He gives power to those who are tired and worn out; he offers strength to the weak. Even youths will become exhausted, and young men will give up. But those who wait on the Lord will find new strength. They will fly high on wings like eagles. They will run and not grow weary. They will walk and not faint"* (Isaiah 40:28-31).

Weary women everywhere! I see them, I listen to them, I look into their tired eyes and wonder how they become so "wearied out" in the first place. Life has surely pounded some of them right into the ground! To others life has apparently been good, but still a weariness invades their personalities.

In the Bible the unweary God speaks to the point, telling us that "even youths will become exhausted" (Isaiah 40:30). The Creator, who is never weary, invites the wearied ones to spend time in his presence; to bathe in the atmosphere of eternal strength; to drink in the air of his power-giving presence—to "wait" long enough to renew their lives. God will mend our raw nerve endings with the stitches of his peace. God's promise to those who look to him for such renewal is that they will not be shamed (Isaiah 49:23).

Are you weary of your weariness? Wouldn't you like to rise above it? Have confidence in the Lord, who can help you soar on wings like the eagle! Start "waiting" today. You can wait on the Lord anytime, anywhere. You can stop internally even as you are busy externally. You can wait on the Lord in a car, in the supermarket, at the playground, or in a meeting. When you feel almost too weary to flap your wings one more time, try "waiting." Soon you'll be competing with the eagle—and soaring high.

Jill Briscoe

From *The One Year Book of Devotions for Women.* Used by permission.

Woman to Woman
- When do you feel truly rested?
- What do you need to do to enjoy the rest that God offers us?

Prayer
Father God, our days feel so short and our to-do list seems so long. The days go by in a blur of errands, work, care, cooking, and cleaning. There is no end of tasks, and there's not even time to just pause and catch our breath. We feel constantly weary with no hope for renewal. And yet, God, you call us to wait on you. You promise us rest—deep, profound, peaceful rest. And your Word says that you always keep your promises. God, help us to find the rest you promise. Help us to look to you, to wait on you, to reflect, to be still and know you are God. And help us to soar with the eagle. In Jesus' name, amen.

Week 5: Fun

Use these activities throughout the week *before* your group meets to discuss this topic and scrapbook together. You'll find that meditating and praying on these topics each day of the week will draw you closer to God and increase your appreciation for his gifts.

Daily Bible Readings

Day 1: Read Psalm 30:11. How has God turned your sorrow to joy?

Day 2: Read Ecclesiastes 5:18-19. What in your life gives you satisfaction? Give thanks to God right now for his gift.

Day 3: Read Job 8:21. How has God filled your mouth with laughter?

Day 4: Read Psalm 37:4. How does God bring delight to us?

Day 5: Read Isaiah 55:1-2. What's the key to lifelong and eternal satisfaction?

Day 6: Read Psalm 5:11-12. How can you be glad in the Lord today?

Family Memory Maker

Choose a night this week to be a family fun night when you'll do whatever your family likes to do for fun. For example, perhaps your family enjoys playing miniature golf, bowling, or playing board games. Serve fun treats, and enjoy spending time together.

Personal Memory Maker

Just for fun, do something silly each day this week. Here are a few ideas to consider. Buy a lipstick in a much brighter color than you normally wear. Play loud praise music, and dance in the living room with your family or roommates. Eat ice cream for breakfast. Talk to one another in pig Latin during dinner one night. Keep a list of all the fun things you do to include in your scrapbook. Thank God for fun, silliness, and laughter.

Scrapbooking Tip

This is a great week to use all your paper scraps. Choose several brightly colored paper scraps, and tear the scraps into smaller pieces. Then use adhesive to attach the paper pieces to your scrapbook page to create a layered confetti look.

Fun

"But let the godly rejoice. Let them be glad in God's presence. Let them be filled with joy" (Psalm 68:3).

Our mother loves the anticipation of planning a fun event, but she can often be a "spur of the moment" type of person as well. As Amy recalls, "Just before I began third grade we moved from Kentucky to Southern California. Mom immediately had us out in the water, learning how to 'jump' the waves and coast along in the surf. But school began, and our beach adventures were soon over for the year. Or so we thought.

"One day Mom picked us up from school. With five kids ranging in age from infant to eight, she had plenty to keep her busy. It's not like she needed any extra hassles in her day. But this day, she started along the road to home, then suddenly exclaimed, 'Let's go to the beach!'

"Did it matter that it was November and there was a bit of a chill in the air? Did it matter that three of us were in school clothes? Did it matter that we had no towels in the car? Of course not! We all agreed with squeals of delight and shouts of affirmation. We were off.

"Within minutes we were at Huntington Beach. 'Roll up your pant legs,' Mom instructed. 'And don't get wet above your knees.'

"We were determined to obey. Until Joel just happened to splash Jill a bit too enthusiastically. Until Amy spied a shell just a bit farther into the water. And so it went until we were drenched at least to our waists or more. Mom waded along the edge of the surf with the two littlest ones, laughing and calling to us.

"Finally it was time to go home. We were shivering with cold and covered with sand. Mom piled us into the car and we headed for home.

"Now, as an adult, I think how much hassle it must have been to later vacuum all that sand out of the car, to clean up after us as we trailed grime and seaweed into the house. I'd be saying, 'I'll never do that again!' But not Mom. We made several more out-of-season, no-towels-handy, I-just-got-a-great-idea trips to the beach or other locations over the years. The joy of it all must have been so immense to Mom that she just couldn't resist."

Are you resisting joy because it's a bit too much trouble? Forget all the extensive planning and jump into action the next time you think of something fun to do. Treat yourself to an afternoon matinee. "Accidentally" open the door of the ice cream parlor instead of the fabric shop. Skip out of the routine and into an outing that will leave a joyous memory in its wake. And watch out for Joel—he's still a bit too enthusiastic in the surf.

Jody Brolsma and Amy Nappa

From *Legacy of Virtue: A Devotional for Mothers.* Used by permission.

Woman to Woman
- What "fun times" do you remember from your childhood?
- What can you do now to simply enjoy the life that God's given you?

Prayer
Dear God, we thank you so much for joy and laughter. Sometimes we are so serious about life with its responsibilities and its sorrows. But you created joy. You gave us life, and you mean for us to enjoy it. God, help us to take time to have fun each day, all the while acknowledging you as the Creator and Giver of this wonderful, precious life. In Jesus' name, amen.

Week 6: Freedom in Christ

Use these activities throughout the week *before* your group meets to discuss this topic and scrapbook together. You'll find that meditating and praying on these topics each day of the week will draw you closer to God and increase your appreciation for his gifts.

Daily Bible Readings
Day 1: Read Galatians 5:13. How can you use your freedom to serve others?
Day 2: Read Romans 8:1-4. How does this truth affect your outlook on life?
Day 3: Read John 8:31-32. How does the truth of Jesus' teaching set you free?
Day 4: Read Isaiah 61:1. What kind of freedom does Christ proclaim? How does that freedom benefit you?
Day 5: Read Ephesians 3:12. What does it mean to approach God freely and fearlessly?
Day 6: Read Galatians 5:1. How can you heed this warning in your life?

Family Memory Maker
Take your children to a pet store to watch the birds in their cages. Talk together about what you think it's like to be those birds in the cages. Then go to a park where you can watch birds that aren't in a cage. Talk together about what you think it's like to be a free bird living in the wild. Then talk about the ways in which people are free. Ask how people's lives are like the lives of birds in the pet store or birds in the park. Ask your children what they think it means to be free in Christ.

Personal Memory Maker
Visit a bookstore, and glance through the titles in the self-help and psychology sections. Make a mental list of all the things that people struggle to overcome. Consider how being free in Christ would affect how a person addresses these issues in life.

When you return home, find a Bible and some string, yarn, or thread, and sit down in a quiet spot. Consider all the things that you struggle to overcome, all the things that hinder you and tie you down. For each of those things, wrap the string around your finger once. Keep going until you can't think of anything else. Then look up and read John 8:36. Notice how your bound finger feels. Unwrap the string, and enjoy the feeling of freedom. Thank God for setting you free. Then ask God to help you live a truly free life.

Scrapbooking Tip
You may find it difficult to find photographs that relate directly to this week's theme. Instead, create a birdcage on your scrapbook page using the template in the back of this book. Let the cage remind you of being enslaved to sin as all of us were before we met Christ. Use a pen and the template to draw the lines of the birdcage on a piece of card stock. Then cut the birdcage out of the card stock, making your cutting line about a quarter of an inch outside the ink lines. Put images that represent enslavement to sin "inside" the birdcage. The cage will cover those images, but you'll know they're there. Use the bird template to make a bird shape. Decorate it to look like you, and position it on the page so it's escaping from the cage. Then put photos on the rest of the page to show the life of freedom that God has called you to. Consider what it means to live in complete freedom—to leave behind a life of enslavement to sin and be free to become all that the Creator intended you to be.

Freedom in Christ

"So if the Son sets you free, you will indeed be free" (John 8:36).

"Is it not clear to you that to go back to that old rule-keeping, peer-pleasing religion would be an abandonment of everything personal and free in my relationship with God? I refuse to do that, to repudiate God's grace. If a living relationship with God could come by rule-keeping, then Christ died unnecessarily" (Galatians 2:21-22, The Message).

In many countries, people live in bondage to evil dictators who are greedy for power. These dictators impose rules that have no rhyme or reason, rules that dominate and impose heavy burdens, rules that take away individuality, creativity, and personal growth. No one is allowed to "become"— only to "do." Such dictatorial governments are based on the fear that if people are given freedom, the dictator will lose power, wealth, and control.

Compare that type of leadership with Christ's. Christ doesn't care about power, wealth, or control. He already has it all by the nature of who he is. His only motivation is love, a love that says, "Here I am. I love you. Choose me if you will. And if you do, the only requirement is that you love me and love others." He came and fought the war; he battled with every power and force and won—by dying. He was our sacrifice for freedom.

Freedom can be heady. After a dictator is toppled, the next difficult task is making sure the citizens don't destroy themselves by going overboard with their new freedom and creating a situation of chaotic anarchy. In the confusion following the end of a dictatorship, another dictator often rises up to impose his own selfish desires on the country. Citizens who aren't sure what freedom really means find themselves back in bondage, which they may find strangely comfortable.

When we receive the freedom from sin that Christ offers, we may feel like the citizens who are suddenly free of an evil dictator. We mustn't fall back into the bondage of sin nor allow the excitement of freedom to overtake our good judgment. Paul warned the church in Galatia about this kind of situation, "It is absolutely clear that God has called you to a free life. Just make sure that you don't use this freedom as an excuse to do whatever you want to do and destroy your freedom. Rather, use your freedom to serve one another in love; that's how freedom grows. For everything we know about God's Word is summed up in a single sentence: Love others as you love yourself. That's an act of true freedom" (The Message).

As followers of Christ, we must remember that freedom is expensive. Jesus gave his life for our freedom. We no longer must live under the bondage of guilt and condemnation; instead, the Holy Spirit lovingly directs and guides us. Don't let the priceless blood of Christ be shed for no reason. And don't let your actions cheapen it. Live no longer as one in bondage—live boldly in the freedom his love gives us!

Sherri Harris

Woman to Woman
- In what ways do you feel free in your life? In what ways do you feel bound?
- What do you think it means to truly experience the freedom that God gives us?

Prayer
Dear God, every good gift comes from you, and one of your greatest gifts is freedom. We are no longer slaves to sin! We can live our lives in freedom. Thank you for giving us such a great gift. Help us to treasure it. We often make the mistake of forgetting we are free and living in the rut of old sin. Help us break free and live the life of love that you have called us to. Help us rely on your Holy Spirit to empower us to become all you mean for us to be. Thank you for loving us so much that you saved us from our sins. In Jesus' name, amen.

Week 7: *God's World*

Use these activities throughout the week *before* your group meets to discuss this topic and scrapbook together. You'll find that meditating and praying on these topics each day of the week will draw you closer to God and increase your appreciation for his gifts.

Daily Bible Readings

Day 1: Read Psalm 19:1-6. How do the heavens declare the glory of God?

Day 2: Read Genesis 1. What made God's creation so good?

Day 3: Read Psalm 148. How does the world around us give praise to God?

Day 4: Read Job 38–39. What does nature tell us about the God who made it?

Day 5: Read Isaiah 55:12-13. What do you see in nature that symbolizes our relationship with God?

Day 6: Read Mark 4:35-41. Consider the power of nature. Why is it so significant that God has power over the wind and the waves?

Family Memory Maker

Visit a local nature area with your family. If you live alone, take a good friend along. If the weather is warm, take a picnic. If the weather is cold or wet, dress warmly and take a walk. If you have young children, help them notice as many things that God created as they can. Take the time to examine each thing they notice. If you have older children, talk about what God's creation teaches you about God. Discuss why it is that so many people feel closer to God when they spend time in nature.

Personal Memory Maker

As you go about your daily routine, pay attention to what God created. For example, maybe you pass a lovely park on your way to work, or perhaps you can see a snowcapped mountain from your bedroom window. As you notice the beauty of God's creation each day, be sure to praise God for his creativity and the beauty of his creation. Consider designing your scrapbook page based on something you observed in God's world this week.

Scrapbooking Tip

Press flowers to include in your scrapbook design this week. Flowers such as daisies, peonies, or roses work well. Cut the stems off and discard them. If you use roses that haven't opened yet, you may want to separate the petals before pressing. Place the blossoms between sheets of white paper, and press them underneath a stack of heavy books for several days. Put the pressed blossoms in plastic sleeves before placing them in your scrapbook.

God's World

> *"He is the God who made the world and everything in it. Since he is Lord of heaven and earth, he doesn't live in man-made temples, and human hands can't serve his needs—for he has no needs. He himself gives life and breath to everything, and he satisfies every need there is. From one man he created all the nations throughout the whole earth. He decided beforehand which should rise and fall, and he determined their boundaries.*
>
> *"His purpose in all of this was that the nations should seek after God and perhaps feel their way toward him and find him—though he is not far from any one of us. For in him we live and move and exist. As one of your own poets says, 'We are his offspring'" (Acts 17:24-28).*

God has revealed himself in many ways. For example, he has shown himself to us in nature. For "from the time the world was created, people have seen the earth and sky and all that God made. They can clearly see his invisible qualities—his eternal power and divine nature. So they have no excuse whatsoever for not knowing God" (Romans 1:20).

As we were talking to some teenagers on the city streets, one said, "Just show me God and I'll believe." The city lay at the gateway to the beautiful English lake district, and I inquired if he ever took a country walk and appreciated the fabulous scenery.

"I know what you're going to say," he said. "You're going to tell me God made all of that! Well, I don't believe in God! I believe it all just happened!"

Taking my watch off my wrist, I opened the back of it and showed the kids the intricate workings. They were duly impressed. "It just happened," I said casually. "One day all the little pieces appeared from nowhere and fell into place inside this little gold case. Then it began to move at just the right pace and told the right time!"

"Do you think we're stupid?" exclaimed one of the boys. "That watch had to have had a maker."

"Right," I answered him. "And so did flowers and trees; and so did you and so did I." He got the point. God's attributes are displayed in his world. Nature is the servant that shows us the master!

Jill Briscoe

From *The One Year Book of Devotions for Women.* Used by permission.

Woman to Woman
- How does nature reveal God to you?
- What about God's world are you most thankful for? Why?

Prayer
Dear God, everything we see in this world reminds us of you. Your power is revealed in the mighty mountains and the pounding sea. The heaviness of fruit trees at harvest time tells of your abundant gifts. God, your glory shines through the golden glow of each sunset. And your faithfulness is praised when the sun rises each new day. Thank you, God, for creating such a beautiful world. And thank you for telling us of yourself in your creation. God, we ask that you help us to look for you and to celebrate you as we appreciate the world we live in. In Jesus' name, amen.

Week 8: My Purpose

Use these activities throughout the week *before* your group meets to discuss this topic and scrapbook together. You'll find that meditating and praying on these topics each day of the week will draw you closer to God and increase your appreciation for his gifts.

Daily Bible Readings

Day 1: Read Micah 6:8. How can we live up to this call?

Day 2: Read 1 Samuel 15:22. Why does God want our obedience?

Day 3: Read Luke 10:27. What does it take to live and love like this every day?

Day 4: Read Romans 8:28. What is God's purpose in making all things work together for good? In what way have we been called according to his purpose?

Day 5: Read 2 Thessalonians 1:11-12. What happens when we live according to our calling? How can we encourage other Christians to fulfill the purpose God has for them?

Day 6: Read Psalm 138:8. How do you think God will work out his plans in your life?

Family Memory Maker

At dinner one night this week, tell one another what you'd like to be when you "grow up." If you have children, tell them how you would have answered this question when you were their age. Tell the others about the dreams you have for your future. Talk about why you each have the dreams you have. How does a sense of purpose play in to your dreams?

Personal Memory Maker

Spend time in prayer and Bible study this week, and ask God about your purpose in life. Write down your interests, your passions, your hopes, and your dreams. Then write a mission statement for your life that sums up what you think is your God-given purpose. For example, perhaps your mission statement would say, "To raise my children to love God with their whole hearts, and to show God's love to all I come into contact with." Consider including your mission statement in your scrapbook pages this week.

Scrapbooking Tip

You may want to have an "Aim for the Stars" theme this week as you create scrapbook pages about your purpose in life. Consider using a midnight blue background paper and drawing gold or silver stars on it with a paint pen. You might have difficulty finding photographs that you'd like to include this week. Consider using pictures of your workplace, your family, your church activities, or your hobbies. You may want to include pictures of missionaries you support. You might write your favorite Bible verses about purpose to include on your page. Or you may want to do journaling on large stars. Another idea is to take a spiritual-gifts inventory (an Internet search for "spiritual gifts" will provide many tests to take) and include the results of the test on your pages.

My Purpose

"And so we keep on praying for you, that our God will make you worthy of the life to which he called you. And we pray that God, by his power, will fulfill all your good intentions and faithful deeds. Then everyone will give honor to the name of our Lord Jesus because of you, and you will be honored along with him. This is all made possible because of the undeserved favor of our God and Lord, Jesus Christ" (2 Thessalonians 1:11-12).

Do you really understand the value of your life, beloved? Do you realize the place you have, the purpose, the influence you have in the way you live? In the relationships you develop? Do you understand the value and impact of your words?

Your life has purpose, dear one. And if you don't think so, it's because you've believed the whispers of the evil one. Don't believe him; he's the father of lies. He's deceiving you with thoughts that, according to 1 Corinthians 2:16, are not according to "the mind of Christ," which was given to you as a child of God.

You've been loved by God, redeemed and created in Christ Jesus unto his good works. Someday you'll stand amazed at how he has used you even when you weren't aware of it.

Make the decision to be available to him each day, to be used as he pleases, and watch what he does.

Kay Arthur

Woman to Woman
- Describe a time you've been surprised and delighted by how God has used you.
- What do you think God's specific purpose for you is?

Prayer
Forgive me, Lord, for thinking you'll use everyone else before you'll use me. Forgive me for not seeing my importance to you and to the work you are doing, for not understanding that my life has a specific purpose. Please remind me to offer myself to your service each day—and then to trust you to lead me step by step, one step at a time. Amen.

Devotion and prayer from *Search My Heart, O God*. Used by permission.

Week 9: Children

Use these activities throughout the week *before* your group meets to discuss this topic and scrapbook together. You'll find that meditating and praying on these topics each day of the week will draw you closer to God and increase your appreciation for his gifts.

Daily Bible Readings

Day 1: Read Psalm 127:3. In what ways are children gifts to their parents, their families and to the community? Why do children bring us such joy?

Day 2: Read Matthew 19:14. Why were children precious to Jesus?

Day 3: Read Proverbs 20:11. What were you known for as a child? What are the children you know known for?

Day 4: Read Isaiah 40:11. How does seeing how tender God is toward the young make you feel?

Day 5: Read Deuteronomy 11:18-19. Why is it so important to teach children?

Day 6: Read 1 John 3:1. Why is it so important that God calls those who believe in him his children?

Family Memory Maker

Play this game with your family this week. Sit in a circle, and take turns around the circle completing this sentence: One great thing about being a child is...Continue until you can't think of anything else. Then tell stories about one another's childhood or babyhood.

Personal Memory Maker

Go to a park where you can watch children playing. While you're watching the children, think about the children you know and what they bring to your life. How are children a gift from God? Then consider your own childhood. What brought you joy? What brought you sorrow? How was your own childhood a gift from God?

Scrapbooking Tip

Whether you have children or not, consider decorating your pages with playful, childlike colors and themes. You may choose pink and blue for a baby theme or choose bright primary colors for a slightly older theme. Also consider hand-lettering this page with thick-tipped markers in a childlike script. If you have children, this is a great place for pictures of your kids. If you don't have children, think about the kids you know, or think about your own childhood, for inspiration for these pages.

Children

"Hear, O Israel! The Lord is our God, the Lord alone. And you must love the Lord your God with all your heart, all your soul, and all your strength. And you must commit yourselves wholeheartedly to these commands I am giving you today. Repeat them again and again to your children. Talk about them when you are at home and when you are away on a journey, when you are lying down and when you are getting up again" (Deuteronomy 6:4-7).

It was a warm sunny day for January in Riverside, California. Two of our five grandchildren were helping us enjoy this fine day. Ten-and-a-half-year-old Christine was helping her Grammy Em plan and cook the dinner. PaPa Bob and Bevan were raking the garden and picking oranges, avocados, and lemons off our trees that surround our property.

As the afternoon progressed, our working men became warm and tired.

Christine said, "Grammy, let's have tea." That's all it takes me to stop whatever I'm doing and put the kettle on for Christine and me to have tea. In the process, we poured the men a tall glass of fresh juice on ice and prepared some yummy-for-the-tummy snacks. We carried the treats up the hill to PaPa and Bevan. How happy they were to receive the refreshment. They thanked us and headed for the bench that sits under a large shady avocado tree overlooking the grounds and our quaint, tree-lined little Rumsey Drive, which winds by our barn.

As Christine and I left them, we headed back toward the house. Christine took my hand and said, "Grammy, I love you." "I love you, too, Christine," I said...

That night as my Bob and I crawled into bed, we began to share about our day with the oh-so-wonderful grandchildren.

"What do a PaPa and seven-year-old grandson talk about on the bench under the big avocado tree?" I asked.

"Oh, very special things," Bob replied. "Boys talk just like you girls talk."

I could still picture PaPa Bob and seven-year-old Bevan—with smudges of dirt on both their faces—sitting on that bench.

Bob continued, "I told Bevan, 'Someday, Bevan, when PaPa's in heaven and you drive down Rumsey Drive as a man, you'll look at this bench we are sitting on and you can remember the day that Grammy Em and sister Christine served us jam and toast with a glass of juice.' Then Bevan said, 'Not only will I remember, but I will bring my son and someday he will bring his son and point to the bench and tell him about the toast and jam we ate on the bench under that big avocado tree over there.' "

How does a little boy understand and think through the process of generations?

How blessed we are to have the God-given opportunity to teach our children and grandchildren about the beauty of God's creations, life and death, and most of all about God the Father, the Son, and God, the Holy Spirit.

Emilie Barnes

From *15 Minutes Alone With God.* Used by permission.

Woman to Woman
• Who made an influence on your faith life as a child?
• Even if you don't have any children of your own, how can you help children to love and know God?

Prayer
Dear Father in heaven, thank you for children. They make us laugh and bring us so much joy. Whenever we are near children our hearts fill to the brim with tenderness and a tremendous longing to nurture them. God, we ask you to help us love the children we are connected to in our daily lives. Help us to be examples to them in our words and our actions so that we may help them know what it means to love you with our whole heart. Help us to regard children as a sacred trust from you. In Jesus' name, amen.

Week 10: *Sisterhood*

Use these activities throughout the week *before* your group meets to discuss this topic and scrapbook together. You'll find that meditating and praying on these topics each day of the week will draw you closer to God and increase your appreciation for his gifts.

Daily Bible Readings

Day 1: Read Ruth 1. How did these women show "sisterhood" to one another?

Day 2: Read Acts 9:36-42. How do women help and support one another? How can you better support the women you know?

Day 3: Read Luke 8:1-3. What can women accomplish when they work together?

Day 4: Read Philippians 4:2. Sometimes "sisters" don't get along. How can we promote unity and friendship between women?

Day 5: Read Luke 10:38-42. Mary and Martha were sisters with different agendas. How can we respond to women whose priorities are different from ours, even when we're sure that we're the ones on the right path?

Day 6: Read Titus 2:3-5. What are some ways older women help younger women today?

Family Memory Maker

Visit the floral department of your local grocery store or discount store, and purchase a variety of flowers. At home, talk with your family about the women who mean a lot to you all. For each woman family members mention, have someone in the family choose a flower to represent her and put it in a vase. Continue until you've placed all the flowers in the vase. Then pray with your family to thank God for these women. Keep the flowers on your kitchen table this week to remind your family to be thankful for these women.

Personal Memory Maker

Purchase a box of pretty stationery. Write a letter to at least one woman whose "sisterhood" has meant a lot to you. Pray for this woman, and ask God to richly bless her. Praise God for bringing such a wonderful woman into your life, and thank him for his wonderful gift. Be sure to send the letter to your friend!

Scrapbooking Tip

Use the pattern on this page and a sheet of acid-free paper to create a string of paper dolls to represent the women who've made a difference in your life. Fold the paper according to the directions shown. Trace the pattern onto the folded paper and cut it out, being sure not to cut through the folds. Unfold the dolls and use adhesive to attach the dolls to your scrapbook. You may want to use a paint pen to write the name of each woman below the paper doll that represents her. You may even want to use pens and paper scraps to decorate each paper doll to look like the woman it represents.

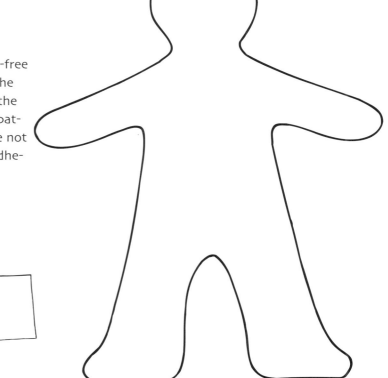

Sisterhood

"Dear friends, since God loved us that much, we surely ought to love each other. No one has ever seen God. But if we love each other, God lives in us, and his love has been brought to full expression through us" (1 John 4:11-12).

How precious are Christian friendships! While we may have many kinds of friends in many different stages and walks of life, friendships with other Christian women can prove to be the most precious because we can share a spiritual bond. We are in tune with each other when we talk about Jesus.

When Jesus talked to his disciples near the end of his life, he explained that they were more than simply followers or servants; they were friends: "I no longer call you servants, because a master doesn't confide in his servants. Now you are my friends, since I have told you everything the Father told me" (John 15:15). That shared knowledge of the Father gave Jesus and the disciples a special depth of friendship.

An essential component of Christian friendship is sharing what we're learning from our heavenly Father about life's experiences. There is nothing that brings you closer to your Christian friends than sharing how God is a comfort in bereavement you didn't expect, a divorce you didn't want, or a sickness you weren't anticipating. Life's lessons learned at the foot of the cross make for deep friendships! Exchanging mutual knowledge of Jesus not only gives you a common focus, it gives you shared secrets to treasure. If your friendships are lacking depth and appear shallow and trivial, try sharing a lesson you are learning about your heavenly Father. If you initiate it, you and your friend will probably soon be chatting away. The time you spend together with your friend will never be time enough!

Jill Briscoe

From *The One Year Book of Devotions for Women.* Used by permission.

Woman to Woman
- Why do women need friendships with other women? How are women uniquely designed to support and care for one another?
- What can you do to develop deeper, more intimate relationships with other women?

Prayer
Dear God, thank you for making women. And thank you for creating women to need friendships with one another. We thank you for the deep bonds that can exist between women who love you and one another deeply. We draw strength and comfort and joy from those bonds. God, help us reach out to others and include them in our circle. Help us love each other deeply, from the heart. We want our love for each other to be real, to be active, to grow and flourish. The friends you have given us are precious gifts. We thank you for them. In Jesus' name, amen.

Week 11: *Family*

Use these activities throughout the week *before* your group meets to discuss this topic and scrapbook together. You'll find that meditating and praying on these topics each day of the week will draw you closer to God and increase your appreciation for his gifts.

Daily Bible Readings
Day 1: Read 1 Timothy 5:8. What responsibilities do we have for our families?
Day 2: Read Galatians 6:10. What responsibilities do we have for our church family?
Day 3: Read Mark 5:18-19. How can we help our families know and love God?
Day 4: Read Micah 7:6. What causes strife in families? What brings healing and peace to relationships?
Day 5: Read 2 Timothy 1:5. How has your family shaped your faith? Who do you consider to be your spiritual parents?
Day 6: Read Luke 15:11-32. What insights into family life does this story teach? What do family members hope for one another?

Family Memory Maker
Spend an evening this week going through family albums and scrapbooks that you've already completed. Tell one another your family stories, and enjoy being together as a family. If you live alone, invite a friend to bring over her family albums, and share your pictures and stories with each other. Talk about what your family means to you and how family can be a gift from God.

Personal Memory Maker
Quickly jot down your family tree on a sheet of paper. How many generations can you include? Consider what you know about your family ancestry. Are there stories or traditions or recipes that have been passed down through the generations in your family? Spend time thinking about what makes your family unique. What can you include in your scrapbook to remind you of your family? Thank God for the things you're thankful for in your family, and ask for God's help for the problems and issues your family faces.

Scrapbooking Tip
Create a "mini" family album to mount in your scrapbook. Take a large sheet of paper, and fold it in half lengthwise. Then fold the paper in half the other way twice. When you unfold the paper, the paper will be divided in eight sections. Fold the paper in half widthwise. Hold the paper by the folded edge. Find the crease that's in the middle of the paper and meets the folded edge perpendicularly. Cut vertically along the crease until you get to the next horizontal crease. Open the paper. Fold the paper lengthwise and push the ends into the middle. Crease all of the fold lines. You'll end up with a small booklet with eight pages. Decorate the front of the booklet to look like a family album. Add small pictures of your family to the inside pages. Attach the booklet to your scrapbook by putting adhesive on the back cover of the booklet.

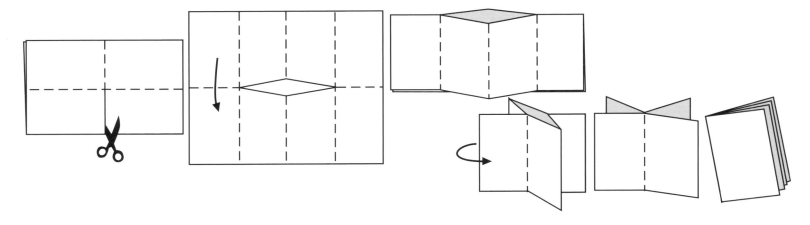

Family

"I pray that out of his glorious riches he may strengthen you with power through his Spirit in your inner being, so that Christ may dwell in your hearts through faith. And I pray that you, being rooted and established in love, may have power, together with all the saints, to grasp how wide and long and high and deep is the love of Christ, and to know this love that surpasses knowledge—that you may be filled to the measure of all the fullness of God" (Ephesians 3:16-19, NIV).

An old European story tells of a traveler in Germany who saw a peculiar sight in a tavern where he had stopped for dinner. After the meal, the tavern owner put a great bowl of soup on the floor and gave a loud whistle. A big dog, a large cat, an old raven, and a very large rat came into the room. They all four went to the dish, and without disturbing each other, ate together. After they had dined, the dog, cat, and rat lay before the fire, while Mr. Raven, in his black coat, hopped around the room. The tavern owner had trained these animals so that not one of them bothered to hurt any of the others. He thought that if a dog, a rat, a cat, and a bird can live happily together, little children, especially brothers and sisters, ought to be able to do the same.

Yes, you would think that harmony could be established in our families, but somehow it escapes us.

In today's passage we find that through Paul's prayer we can learn some basic principles for praying for our own family.

1. *Pray that your family may be rooted and established in love.* Oh, how we need families that really love each other. We see so much evil that originates from the family. Ask God to protect your family from evil and put a hedge of protection around each member.

2. *Pray that you may have power to grasp how wide and long and high and deep is the love of Christ.* Today there is a lack of commitment, a lack of trust, a lack of love in relationships. Pray that your family may begin to grasp the vastness in Christ's love for them individually and collectively.

3. *Pray that your family may know this love that surpasses knowledge.* We cannot comprehend this love that gives beyond our knowledge. But with a great leap of faith, we believe and live the gospel message first within our own life and then share with our family members this love.

4. *Pray that you will be filled in measure of all the fullness of God.* Each day that I'm in God's Word, I better understand what the fullness of God is all about. After many years of life, I better understand being filled in measure of God's fullness. And being in his family is so much a part of that fullness. Proverbs 24:3-4 states, "By wisdom a house is built, and through understanding it is established; through knowledge its rooms are filled with rare and beautiful treasures" (NIV).

Emilie Barnes

From *15 Minutes Alone With God*. Used by permission.

Woman to Woman

- As a child, did you have a family that nurtured your faith? Why or why not? How do our families affect our relationship with God?
- How can you help those in your family love God more?

Prayer

Dear God, we know that families are important to you. We who believe in you call you Father, and you call us your beloved children. We know that's no accident. There's a special relationship that grows between those who are in the same family. Please help us as we live together with our families here in this world. Help us to love our children, our spouses, our parents, and our grandparents with your love. Dear Father, we want to help those we love to love you more and to be pictures of the relationship we have with you. In your Son's precious name, amen.

Week 12: *My Relationship With God*

Use these activities throughout the week *before* your group meets to discuss this topic and scrapbook together. You'll find that meditating and praying on these topics each day of the week will draw you closer to God and increase your appreciation for his gifts.

Daily Bible Readings

Day 1: Read 1 John 3:1. How does this truth affect your relationship with God?

Day 2: Read 1 John 4:7-21. Describe the life that God's children live.

Day 3: Read Psalm 16:8. How does this truth affect how you feel about God?

Day 4: Read Acts 17:24-27. How does knowing that God wants to have a relationship with you make you feel?

Day 5: Read Isaiah 43:1-2. How does God's presence in your life affect you?

Day 6: Read Psalm 139:17-18, 23-24. What do these verses say to you about the kind of relationship you can have with God?

Family Memory Maker

One night at dinner, ask your family, "What does it mean to be friends with God?" Talk together about your human friendships and how they are similar to and different from friendship with God. Be sure your children know how to begin a relationship with God, if they haven't already. It involves confessing their sins, asking God to forgive them, and believing that Jesus lived a perfect life and died on the cross to save them from their sins. Beginning a relationship with God means giving their lives to God and letting God be in control.

Personal Memory Maker

Spend time one day this week meditating on all the roles that God plays in our lives. Here are some roles to get you started: Redeemer, Comforter, Counselor, and Lord. Consider how your life is enriched by God's presence in it. Consider how you are in relationship with God. Then make a point to pay attention to God's presence in your life daily.

Scrapbooking Tip

Use the cross template in this book to create a word mosaic. First, make a list of words that you associate with your relationship with God. For example, your words might include *peace* or *guidance* or *friend*. Then lay the cross template on a piece of decorative paper. Write the words inside the space, adding visual interest by arranging the words in different directions, using different colors, and adding doodles or drawings. Use scissors with a decorative edge to cut out the cross shape and add it to your scrapbook.

My Relationship With God

"For the Lord your God has arrived to live among you. He is a mighty savior. He will rejoice over you with great gladness. With his love, he will calm all your fears. He will exult over you by singing a happy song" (Zephaniah 3:17).

Have you yearned for someone to take you by the hand and walk you safely through the traumas of life? Do you long to rest in someone's arms?

In each of us there is a longing for the spiritual. And we're never more aware of it than when we come up against something we cannot control. Dear one, there is One who is always available to listen, to guide, and to mark your life with the imprint of his own. God wants to speak to your heart right now through his Word and by his Spirit. Won't you spend time with him, praying and reading his Word, letting him speak to you?

Look at Psalm 27:8 (NASB). It says, "When you said, 'seek my face,' my heart said to you, 'Your face, O Lord, I shall seek.' "

Precious one, will you put your hand in his in childlike trust? He's reaching out to you today, eager to walk by your side through all of life's trials. He's reminding you that his everlasting arms are ready to sustain you.

Kay Arthur

Woman to Woman

- How do you see God? Is God a parent? a friend? a judge? a protector? a lover? or something else?
- Do you feel like you know God intimately, as a best friend? What can you do to become better friends with God?

Prayer

Dear heavenly Father, I need to feel your loving presence here beside me, walking with me through this difficult day. Speak to my heart as I wait in silence, meditating on your Word. Give me the peace only you can give. In Jesus' name, amen.

Devotion and prayer from *Search My Heart, O God*. Used by permission.

God's Good Gifts

A Scrapbooking Bible Study for Women's Groups

Group's Scripture Scrapbook™

Group

Loveland, Colorado

Group resources actually work!

This Group resource helps you focus on **"The 1 Thing™"**—a life-changing relationship with Jesus Christ. "The 1 Thing" incorporates our **R.E.A.L.** approach to ministry. It reinforces a growing friendship with Jesus, encourages long-term learning, and results in life transformation, because it's:

Relational
Learner-to-learner interaction enhances learning and builds Christian friendships.

Experiential
What learners experience through discussion and action sticks with them up to 9 times longer than what they simply hear or read.

Applicable
The aim of Christian education is to equip learners to be both hearers and doers of God's Word.

Learner-based
Learners understand and retain more when the learning process takes into consideration how they learn best.

God's Good Gifts
A Scrapbooking Bible Study for Women's Groups
Leader Guide

Pages 3-15 Copyright © 2004 Sherri Harris
Pages 17-28 Copyright © 2004 Group Publishing, Inc.

Visit our Web site: **www.group.com**

Credits
Creative Development Editor: Matt Lockhart
Chief Creative Officer: Joani Schultz
Editor: Beth Robinson
Copy Editor: Alison Imbriaco
Art Director: Kari K. Monson
Cover Art Director: Jeff A. Storm
Photographer: Rodney Stewart
Production Manager: Peggy Naylor

10 9 8 7 6 5 4 3 2   13 12 11 10 09 08 07

Printed in Malaysia.

Contents

Introduction 4

Leading a Scripture Scrapbook Group 7

Supply List 15

Endorsements 17

Practical Tips for Leading Small Groups 19

Welcome to *God's Good Gifts*—the third book

in Group's Scripture Scrapbooks™ series. This book will provide another opportunity for you and a small group of women to bring your memories together with God's Word for a time of fellowship, study, introspection, and meditation.

The more we grow in our relationships with God, the more we realize how good God has been to us. God gives us so many good gifts every day. You'll spend the next twelve weeks celebrating God's gracious and generous nature. You'll discover just how much God loves you as you think about how he's blessed your life through your family, your friends, and your church and by the way he's specially created you to be a unique and wonderful woman. In this book, you'll explore these gifts from God:

- Myself
- Church
- Home
- Rest
- Fun
- Freedom in Christ
- God's World
- My Purpose
- Children
- Sisterhood
- Family
- My Relationship With God

It is our hope that you'll have both a greater appreciation for yourself and a greater appreciation for your Lord and Creator at the end of this time together. Enjoy building friendships with other women, and don't be afraid to fully enjoy discovering who you are and who you can be through the Holy Spirit.

This book includes devotions, Scriptures, and prayers to help you discover all you can about God's good gifts to you. It also includes memory-making activities to do with your family and friends, activities to help you make memories with God, and scrapbooking tips and ideas. The book suggests a Scripture reading for each day of the week leading up to your group meeting. These Scriptures will deepen your understanding of the topic and help you get the most from your discussions with your friends.

Have fun with this book, and may it help you better love yourself, others, and the God who made you!

Leading a Scripture Scrapbook Group

Here are some tips for negotiating your way through the *who, when, where, why,* and *how* of successfully leading a Scripture Scrapbook group.

Who

God's Good Gifts: A Scrapbooking Bible Study for Women's Groups is a wonderful choice for any group of women who want to build deep, lasting friendships and grow closer to God.

This project can be used with women who have been studying the Bible together for years or with women who have never studied the Bible before. It can be used by women whose friendships stretch back for many years, and by women who are just beginning to get to know one another. This project could be used with a group of teenage girls, and it would be just as successful in a group of grandmothers. This project could be used with the women from your church, women from churches all over your community, or women from your neighborhood. The discussion, the insights, and the Christian growth will be unique to each group of women that goes through this project.

The project is also adaptable to any size group. It has been tested with a small group of five women, as well as with a group of over thirty-five women. It worked great in both groups! You'll find tips sprinkled throughout this Leader Guide to help you make this project a success with your group.

For example, you should plan to have one leader or facilitator for each group of five women. If you have multiple groups of five, have each group of five women sit at one table and do this project as a small group. Consider having the same small groups of women sit together for the duration of this project. The women will experience much deeper intimacy if they study, pray, and work as a small group throughout this project.

When

You'll need to plan for a two-hour session each week to give your group a comfortable time frame for Bible study, prayer, fellowship, and scrapbooking. You might choose to begin each session with coffee and a snack.

Plan on this project lasting thirteen weeks. You'll need one session at the beginning to introduce the project and make plans. During the first session, make sure each woman has a participant book. Give each woman the list of supplies from page 15 of this book. Decide together whether each woman will bring her own scrapbooking materials or if the leader will be providing the materials. If the group decides to have the leader supply the materials, be sure to discuss how the leader will be reimbursed for the materials.

Have the women take note of the topic for the next week. The first topic is "Myself." Explain that, for the session, each woman will need to bring photographs that tie in to the topic of "Myself" for her scrapbook.

Show the women page 9 of the participant guide. There are Scripture readings and activities the women may want to do during the week preceding each meeting. For example, encourage the women to do as much of the "Week 1: Myself" activities before you meet to do the devotion (Participant Guide, page 9) and scrapbook together.

Make sure everyone understands and agrees to support one another and to demonstrate Christian friendship and love for the others in the group. The women in the group should be expected to keep confidences and be loyal to one another. Every woman should understand that her participation in the discussion is strongly encouraged and hoped for in the spirit of friendship but that no one will be expected to share that which is painful, embarrassing, or uncomfortable.

At that first meeting, you'll also need to discuss the schedule for the project. You'll need twelve weeks for the actual project. Be sure to be sensitive to holidays, school vacations, and special church or community events. Be flexible and plan around those special times.

Where

If you're doing this project with a small group of women (about five), you can comfortably do it around your kitchen table. If you have a larger group of women, you'll need a bigger space. Plan on having one large table for every five women. You may need to use your church's fellowship hall if you have a really large group. Be sure to plan in advance so you'll find a location that'll be just right for your group.

Why

As a leader, do your best to help your group remember that this project isn't a talent contest to see who is the most creative. It's an opportunity for women to put their own memories into action in their spiritual walk. It is also an opportunity for women to share God's work and his faithfulness with their families.

Nevertheless, the scrapbooks will be lasting treasures. One great idea is to present a finished scrapbook as a family gift. One woman collected pictures from siblings and made one to give to her mother for Mother's Day. Another woman made scrapbooks for her mother and mother-in-law as Christmas gifts. The scrapbooks proved to be something they each treasure.

How

First, let's talk about how to lead the devotion. Then we'll talk about how to do the scrapbooking. Last, we'll talk about building community and developing relationships among women.

The Devotion—Each week you'll study a topic and then scrapbook on that same topic. For example, the first week you'll have a devotion on the topic of "Myself," and then you'll scrapbook pages about yourself.

To begin the devotion portion of your time together, open with prayer.

Then have someone read aloud the Scripture passage at the top of the page and the devotion that follows. You may want to do the reading

yourself, or you may prefer to choose someone from your group who reads well and expressively.

Next, read aloud and discuss each of the questions under the heading "Woman to Woman." As the leader, you might consider getting the discussion going by sharing your own experiences. It's important that the group leader be open and vulnerable to her group. Others won't be open to sharing their own thoughts and feelings if there is not that openness and trust from the group leader. Be sure you don't rush the discussion—allow time for women to learn and grow in their Christian walk. Use the discussion time to help women learn from one another's insights and experiences.

Encourage everyone to participate, and work to create a warm, safe environment that will make people comfortable. Don't allow one person to dominate the discussion.

Occasionally you may find that someone is unusually quiet or reluctant to share during the discussion time. It may be that the day's topic or the woman's memories are too close to the heart to be shared. That's OK. Don't pressure anyone to share what is uncomfortable, but be positive, and keep the discussion moving and on the right track.

The topics covered in the devotions may evoke strong emotions. That's OK. We often learn the most when we feel strongly. As the leader, you might not know how to respond to someone who becomes very emotional or brings up a traumatic experience. Don't feel pressured to say the perfect thing. It's much more important for people to feel comfort, love, and acceptance. You may want to offer comfort by putting your hand on the woman's shoulder or by taking her hand in your own, but remember that some people are uncomfortable being touched. Never judge or condemn another's emotions, and don't make anyone feel that she should be more spiritual or "above" such responses.

An emotional response might bring the perfect moment to ask the woman if you could pray for her. You may want to open up this prayer time so the entire group can pray for their sister in Christ. In your prayer, thank God for being so loving. Thank God for working to bring healing to this pain or loss. Thank God for giving this woman courage and strength to work toward healing. Ask God to give comfort and strength for this moment and for the next few days and weeks. Ask God to give direction, wisdom, and desire to move forward.

When you have finished praying, continue to be compassionate and kind, but don't make the woman feel uncomfortable or dig for more facts. Allow the discussion to come back to a comfortable level. If you feel this person needs further help, just pull her aside later or give her a call the next day. Let her know that you appreciate her. Help her seek out whatever help she needs. Perhaps you could send her a card, thanking her for being honest, and encourage her with Scripture and kind words.

Here's another situation you might encounter. You might find during this project that a woman is unsure about her relationship with Jesus. Consider it a privilege to talk with her about what it means to be a Christian. It would probably be best to contact her outside of your regular meeting time—that will give the two of you the time and privacy you need to talk. If you're unsure about how to introduce Jesus to someone, ask your pastor for help.

After the discussion has progressed for about thirty minutes, transition into your scrapbooking time. Tell the women that the discussion may continue as they begin to crop their pictures and decorate their pages. You'll come back to the prayer section of the devotion after scrapbooking.

Scrapbooking—To spark scrapbooking creativity, suggest that everyone take a look at the idea pages in the participant guide. They'll provide lots of guidance and fresh ideas for what can be done with this project.

Those who have past experience scrapbooking will probably be fine without too much help or guidance. There might be some who need help with this process, especially the first three to four sessions. It might be wise for you, as the leader, to have your pictures prepared ahead of time so you can help those who need it.

The devotions in the participant guide are designed to be torn out and placed in each woman's scrapbook. The devotions will make one of the two pages that participants will create each session.

Each week, the participants should bring photos that have to do with the week's topic. The women can look ahead to see what the next topic is and how many photos they'll need. They may want to have their photos duplicated before they come so that the originals are maintained. Some may also want to enlarge or reduce their photos to fit into a particular space in their books.

Thank you, Lord, for creating me.

The templates provided in the participant guide will help women create the second of the two pages they'll make each week. The templates are designed to lie on top of the photos so it's easy to see what to cut out. It's best to use a wax pencil designed for drawing on photos. Then the excess can be wiped off with a tissue after  cutting. Make sure the women lay out all the pictures so they can see how the page will look before they actually cut any of the pictures.

You'll also find pages of stickers in the back of the participant guide to help each woman decorate her pages.

When it looks like the pages are complete or when time is coming to an end, start asking each woman, one at a time, to hold up her book. Be sure to allow enough time for this—about thirty minutes. Each person can share why she chose the pictures on her page and how they relate to the topic of the day.

You'll find that sometimes the pages are fun and frivolous; other times they are deeply rooted with meaning. This is where you really see and begin to understand a part of each person and have insight into her life.

After each one has shared her page with the group, have someone read the prayer from the bottom of the devotion. Our group found that this was such an incredible summary of all we had discussed, and it brought everything to an appropriate closing point.

Building community—Being part of a small group for this time period means that you will journey through a variety of life experiences. Maybe someone in your group will get married or have a baby. Celebrate with her! You may want to have a party or throw a shower for her one week. Maybe someone will experience a tragedy. Grieve with her and comfort her!

Take meals to one another when doing so would ease a heavy load. Send cards of encouragement. Get together on occasions other than your regular scrapbooking day. Call one another on the phone. Send e-mails. Get to know one another's families. Pray for one another. Share one another's burdens. Love one another with the love of Christ.

This group is about sharing memories, but it is also about sharing stories of life experiences and building friendships that will last for eternity. Help one another by sharing in the happy moments, as well as supporting one another in difficult times. We must learn to literally love our neighbor as our self. That's the great commandment, second only to loving our Lord God with all our hearts, minds, and souls.

Supply List

The supplies each participant will need are:

- ❑ *God's Good Gifts* participant book
- ❑ 8½x11 or 12x12 scrapbook
- ❑ scissors
- ❑ tape runner or acid-free adhesive of some kind
- ❑ wax pencil (to draw on photos)

Other supplies that can be used are:

- ❑ a straightedge paper cutter (for greater precision on photos)
- ❑ decorative paper or card stock
- ❑ decorative scissors
- ❑ decorative pens
- ❑ stickers
- ❑ die cuts
- ❑ rubber stamps and stamp pads
- ❑ anything else each participant would choose to make her scrapbook exclusively hers!

Remember, these scrapbooks are keepsakes! They are for each individual to cherish and hold dear. They don't need to be replicas of someone else's, unless that is what a participant chooses. They can be decorated without a lot of expense, and extras can always be added later.

Endorsements

"As an avid 'scrapbooker,' I love *Christian Living From A to Z*! The pages I create are deeply satisfying. Choosing pictures and the journaling that follows bring me closer to God than any Bible study I have done so far!"

—*Jessica Branaugh*

"This study has allowed me to create a 'window into my soul' for my kids. It also lets me focus on building characteristics that are pleasing to the Lord."

—*Lisa Walsh*

"*Christian Living From A to Z* has been such a unique way to see God's presence in my life. Viewing my pictures and memories from God's Word has given me a renewed love and appreciation for God's faithfulness."

—*Lisa Bernhardt*

"This book has given me a wonderful opportunity to focus on a small window of my life each week. I am able to see God's love and faithfulness to me and be encouraged to pour that love out on those around me. The added bonus is the satisfaction of creating something unique and beautiful."

—*Kathy Ichiyasu*

Practical Tips for Leading Small Groups

Before the Meeting

1. One of the most important things you can do to ensure a positive group experience is to pray for the members of your group through the week. Keep the group prayer list in a conspicuous place: on the refrigerator door, in your car, in your Bible or journal, in your PDA, or taped to your bathroom mirror.

2. Even though *Group's Scripture Scrapbooks™: God's Good Gifts* is designed to be led with minimal prep time, take some time to preview the devotion during the week. Ask God to give you insight into the devotion so that you might lead the group to know and understand God more.

3. Before your group is scheduled to meet, make sure the meeting environment is appropriate. Is the temperature comfortable? Do you have enough chairs? Is the table big enough? How's the lighting? Do you have all the supplies you will need (extra pens, Bibles, adhesive, scissors, decorative papers)? What about refreshment supplies (plates, cups, napkins, ice, hot water, coffee)? Is the bathroom presentable, and is there toilet paper? All of these details are important components of a good meeting.

Pre-meeting checklist:
__ temperature
__ seating arrangement
__ work space
__ lighting
__ supplies for the meeting
__ supplies for refreshments
__ bathroom
__ other: _____

4. Prior to the start of your time together, make an effort to personally welcome and greet each person as she arrives.

5. Have refreshments available at the start of the meeting. Build in ten to fifteen minutes of snack time before moving into the devotion. This way people who might be running a few minutes late won't miss the start of the lesson.

During the Devotion

1. As much as possible, do what you can to not let the devotion time be interrupted. One obvious interruption is phone calls. If practical, don't answer the phone. Also, at the start of the devotion, ask people to turn off or down cell phones and pagers. If your phone number is an emergency contact number for the group, arrange ahead of time for a designated person to answer the phone.

2. Always start on time. If you are faithful about starting on time from the first meeting, you'll discourage people from arriving and starting later and later as the study goes on.

3. At times you may be tempted to skip the devotion and move right into the scrapbooking time. Avoid this temptation. The devotion is the time women in your group will really explore their relationships with God. Though the discussion during the scrapbooking time can be deeply spiritual, your group is sure to benefit from concentrated time thinking about God's truths together.

4. As valuable as the devotion is, try to move into the scrapbooking part of your meeting on schedule. The women need to have plenty of time to finish their pages at the meeting. Otherwise, you'll find the frustration level rising as you move on to the next topic before the current project is finished.

5. Be willing to pray at times other than the closing prayer time. Prayer is a powerful tool and can be helpful in setting the proper tone. For example, bless the food. Praying at the start of the lesson is a good way to let everyone know the session is starting.

6. If you have a large group (eight or more), don't be afraid to break into smaller groups. See this as an opportunity for greater participation by everyone in the group, as well as an opportunity to recognize and encourage leadership in others.

7. Be sensitive to giving everyone an opportunity to participate, but at the same time, be careful not to put anyone on the spot. Let the group members know upfront that they are free to pass on any question

they're not comfortable answering.

8. Try not to talk too much. Don't feel as if you always have to share first or give the last word. Think of yourself as a facilitator—one who encourages everyone to join in the discussion. Avoid the natural impulse to fill a few uncomfortable seconds of silence. Silence can be a tool you use to allow people an opportunity to share. Also, without being pushy, you can gently prompt someone to share by asking, "What do you think?"

9. Keep the group on track. Encourage good discussion, but don't be timid about calling time on a given question and moving on. Part of your job is clock management. If the group decides to spend extra time on a given question or activity, consider skipping or spending less time on a later question or activity in order to stay on schedule.

10. Always be sure to allow enough time to close in prayer, and make sure someone writes down the group's prayer requests. (See the Prayer Ministry Coordinator description on page 27.) Prayer is one of the most important things your group can experience together. (For a variety of ways to pray in your group, see pages 24-25.)

11. Before dismissing the group, confirm the time and place of your next gathering. Make sure that whoever is responsible for refreshments at the next meeting is aware of her responsibility.

12. End on time. Even if not everyone has finished her pages, call time when the clock rolls around to the stated or advertised ending time, and give women in the group the opportunity to leave if they need to. Then proceed to wrap up as quickly as you can. By doing this you communicate that you value and respect people's time and that you are a person of your word.

After the Meeting

1. Be prepared for people to want to hang out and talk after the meeting. If for any reason you (or the host) need people to leave by a certain time, be sure to make this clear during the meeting.

2. Thank people for coming, and let them know that you look forward to seeing them again at the next meeting.

3. If there was someone in the group who was facing a particular need or issue this week, make plans to follow up with a call, card, visit, or e-mail.

4. You'll also find it helpful to take a minute to assess how the meeting went by asking yourself the following questions: (1) How did it go? (2) What could have been better? (3) What should we continue to do or stop doing? (4) Is there anything or anyone with whom I need to follow up?

5. On occasion, plan to call or send a note, card, or e-mail to the members in your group for no reason other than to say hello and to let them know that you are praying for them.

Easy Ways to Promote Your Group

Before you begin this Bible study project, you'll want to promote the opportunity in your church, your neighborhood, and your community. Here are some great tips:

1. Advertise your group through your church. Use all available means—the church bulletin and newsletter, bulletin boards, the church Web site, and announcements during the service. Additional creative approaches that you or group members might consider include hosting an information table before and after services, contacting recent visitors, and letting the church staff—pastoral and administrative—know about your group.

2. Don't overlook the power of a personal invitation. Invite people you know from work or church.

3. Advertise in the local paper.

4. Before officially launching your group, hold an initial "no obligation" sneak-preview meeting of inquiry. Give an overview of what the group will be studying and doing.

5. As a group, canvass the neighborhood where your group meets.

Deliver baked goods along with invitations to check out your group.

6. Ask already-committed group members to post fliers around their workplaces, as their company policies permit, with information about the group and their names and numbers as contacts for more information.

7. As a group, focus on reaching out to visitors to your church. Have a one-page information sheet that group members can give to any visitors they meet.

8. As part of your personal prayer time, pray that God would bring people to the group.

Six Child-Care Solutions

A challenging issue for many groups is child care. This may or may not be an issue you face personally. But if it is an issue for someone in your group, I encourage you to think of it as your problem and to take the lead in offering solutions and options. (See Luke 9:48.) Child care, or the lack thereof, can be the difference between whether or not someone engages in Christian community. Here are some ideas that may work for your group.

1. Perhaps the easiest approach is to have everyone take responsibility for her own child-care arrangements. However, it's a good idea to make child care a group concern. This issue gives the group an opportunity early on to practice community.

2. If your meeting area is conducive to this, have participants bring their children to the meeting, and have on-site child care available that mothers can pay for on a child-by-child basis.

3. If most or all of the members of the group have young children, allow the group members to serve one another by rotating child-care responsibilities in the group. Ideally,

A special note regarding child care: It is wise to prescreen any potential child-care worker—paid or volunteer—who is watching children as part of a church-sanctioned activity (including a home Bible study). Your church may already have a screening process in place that your group can use.

this child care would be on-site where the group is meeting.

4. If there are members in your group with older children who are mature enough to watch the younger children, pay these kids to watch, or even put on a lesson for, the younger kids during the meeting.

5. Check to see if your church's youth group would be interested in providing child care as a youth-group fundraiser. Be mindful that any young person who watches children should be certified, screened, and under adult supervision.

6. Consider having your group meet at the church during a time child care is already available. If child care is available for a time period that's shorter than your group's normal meeting time, adjust your meeting time to fit the child-care schedule, or make other arrangements.

Fourteen Approaches to Group Prayer

Modeling prayer as you lead your group is very important, *especially* in a group that is meeting for the first time. Don't assume that people will be comfortable praying out loud. And be careful not to call on someone to pray out loud unless you know ahead of time that she is comfortable doing so.

Introducing different ways to pray during the weeks your group meets is one way to help women in your group experience prayer. Here are several ideas to get you started:

1. For a first meeting where people may not know one another well, take prayer requests, and then you, as the leader, should offer a closing prayer. To solicit prayer requests, ask, "How can this group pray for you this week?"

2. One way to learn who in your group is comfortable praying aloud is simply to ask for volunteers. During your second meeting, ask, "Who would like to close us in prayer today?" Then take prayer requests, and have your volunteers pray.

3. A great way to get a larger group to pray together is to divide up into pairs. Have the people focus on praying for each other.

4. Another way to pray in a group is to give everyone a sentence to complete for short, simple sentence prayers. For example, ask everyone to complete one of the following sentences: "Lord, I want to thank you for…" or "Lord, I want to pray for…"

5. Don't overlook the power of silent prayer. Close with a time of silent prayer.

6. Another way to encourage silent prayer is to pause briefly (for ten seconds or so) after each prayer request to allow the group to pray for that request before moving on to the next request. Brief pauses can be more effective than a longer period of silence that comes at the end of a long list of requests.

7. A group can pray around a prayer circle. Form a circle, and have everyone take a turn praying. If you do this, make it clear that silent prayer is an option. A person who prays silently can squeeze the hand of the person she is next to in order to let the person know when she has finished.

8. Pray Scripture together. The Lord's Prayer is a good choice, as are selected psalms. This can be done all together or by breaking up the passage into parts. This form of scripted prayer will make praying aloud easier for some.

9. Have an open prayer time when anyone who wants to can offer up a prayer or prayers. You'll find it helpful to designate a person to open the prayer time and a person to close the prayer time.

10. Ask everyone to "pray for the person to your right or left—silently or aloud." If someone chooses to pray silently, ask her to say amen at the end of the prayer so the next person knows she has finished.

11. Pray in the form of singing a common chorus or hymn, such as the doxology.

12. Read a prayer from the Bible—for example, John 17:20-26.

13. Read a prayer in your group from a book of prayers.

14. To make the prayer time special for a final session or meeting, have the group stand together in a circle. Then have each member of

the group take a turn standing or, if comfortable, kneeling in the center of the group as the group prays specifically for that person.

Four Helpful Tools

The following simple tools can go a long way in enhancing the effectiveness of your group. Pick and choose which tools you think would be helpful to your group.

1. A printed prayer list—Don't underestimate the power of a simple prayer list. At each meeting, everyone should receive a copy of a prayer list that shows the names of all the group's members and their current prayer requests. The prayer list can be a powerful tool as group members see God move in response to the requests.

2. Refreshment sign-up sheet—Not as powerful as the prayer list, but important nonetheless, *especially* if you don't want to be stuck doing refreshments week after week just because you forgot to ask. Remember, a fed group is a happy group!

3. Contact-information master list—Put together a list that includes members' names, addresses, phone numbers, and e-mail addresses. Gather this information when you first meet, and update accordingly as new people join the group. Make copies, and distribute them to the members of the group. This is a helpful tool that members can reference when they want to mail a card of encouragement, call, or e-mail someone with a prayer request. Be clear upfront about how this list may be used, as some people may not want to or be allowed to receive personal calls or e-mails at work.

4. Church directory—If your church has a pictorial directory, plan to keep one handy. I encourage you to view your group as part of the greater ministry of your church. As women in your group pray as a group for needs in your church, they might find it helpful to see pictures so they know for whom they are praying.

Six Ways to Maximize Participation

One way to increase the level of connectedness in your group is to give people an area of ministry that they can own. Not everyone in your group will want to take on a responsibility, but others will welcome the opportunity. Keep the following list of ministry positions in mind as you think of ways to encourage involvement in the life of the group.

These suggested ministry responsibilities can be assigned for the length of the study or on a rotating basis.

1. Prayer Ministry Coordinator—Have someone who is passionate about prayer be the keeper of the prayer list and the spark plug when the group needs to know about special urgent prayer needs that arise between group meetings.

2. Meeting Host—While the leader of a group oftentimes also serves as the meeting host, a way to further involve others in the group is to have someone other than you host the meeting. Coordinating some of the meeting details might require an effort on your part, but allowing someone else to host will give her the opportunity to serve in the area of her giftedness. The responsibility of hosting the meetings can also be rotated. However, *especially* for new groups, I recommend a standard gathering spot, at least until the people in the group get to know one another better.

3. Subgroup Leader(s)—Depending on the size of your group, you may find it very helpful and practical to break into smaller groups. This is a great opportunity to utilize other leaders in the group, as well as to help develop future leaders by having them serve as subgroup discussion facilitators.

4. Food Coordinator—A seemingly minor detail, refreshments can become an unnecessary distraction for the leader of a group. However, recognize that food is an important ingredient of a successful group. Where there is food, there is fellowship. Give someone the opportunity

to coordinate this aspect of the group.

5. Child-Care Coordinator—As mentioned earlier, child care can be a big issue for a group. Let someone with the contacts, know-how, and a heart for kids help address this vital issue.

6. Care Coordinator—Over the course of a group's time together, specific needs within the group inevitably will arise. For example, someone may fall ill and be in need of meals. Or the group may want to send a card of encouragement. Have a person be in charge of the details associated with these needs, such as picking up birthday and get-well cards that the group can send and arranging for meals.

Three Suggested Ground Rules

The ideal *Group's Scripture Scrapbooks*™ group is one in which people experience true Christian community. To help achieve this end, setting forth a few simple rules upfront can be helpful.

1. Confidentiality—As a general rule, what is shared in the group stays in the group. Notable exceptions: (1) If permission is sought and granted to share a story beyond the group. (2) If a person is believed to be a threat to herself or to another.

2. Commitment—While recognizing that not everyone will always be able to make every meeting, the group is encouraged to make full participation a high priority during the life of the group.

3. Christ-Centeredness—The ultimate mission of the group is to encourage people to grow in their relationship with Christ.

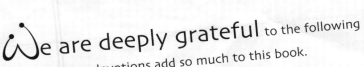

Ꞷe are deeply grateful to the following women whose devotions add so much to this book.

Kay Arthur

Emilie Barnes

Jill Briscoe

Jody Brolsma

Sherri Harris

Amy Nappa